Created with Emotions

AUBREY COLEMAN

Created with Emotions

www.thedailygraceco.com

STUDY CONTRIBUTORS

Illustrator
KATIE LINSTRUM

Editors
JANA WHITE
ALLI TURNER

God created you with every little detail.

He created you with your color of eyes.

He created you with the perfect number of hairs on your head.

He created you with a huge imagination.

He created you with arms to give big hugs.

And He created you with emotions!

Emotions tell us what we feel in our hearts.

Emotions tell us how we feel about things going on around us.

Do we feel joy? Do we feel anger? Do we feel sadness?

We feel them because of something we see, hear, say, remember, or do.

We feel emotions in our minds and bodies.

If we are nervous, our hearts might beat really fast.

When we feel sad, tears might fall from our eyes.

If we are joyful, we might smile from ear to ear!

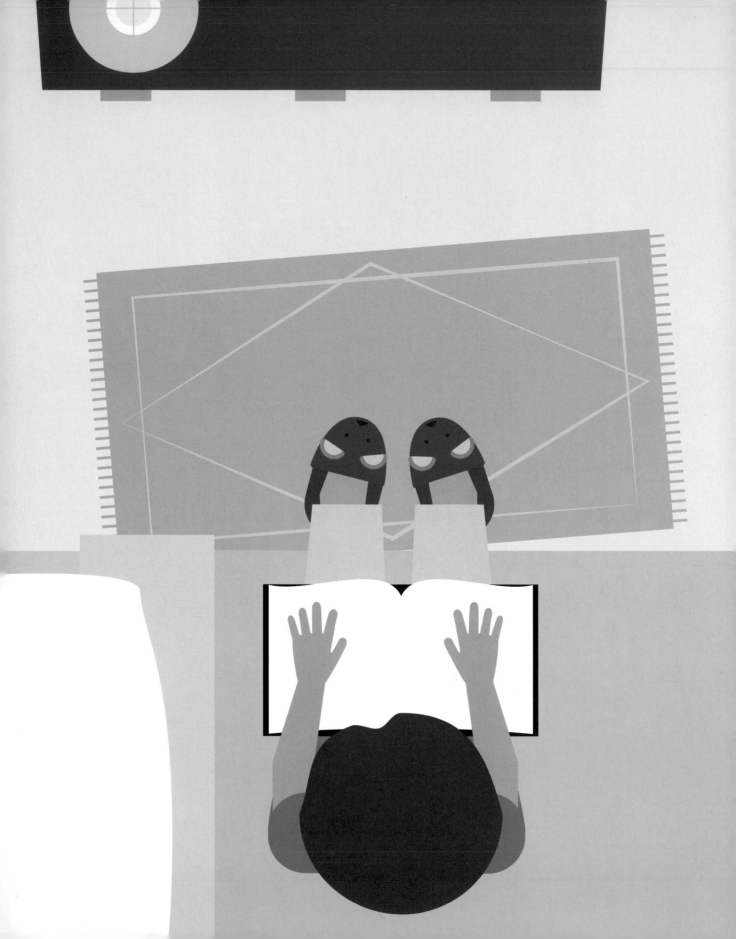

Did you know that God has emotions?

In the Bible, God expresses joy, anger, jealousy, grief, and love.

But God is holy, and His emotions are perfect.

God is never tricked or confused by sin.

His emotions are always used for His glory and the good of others.

Everything God creates is good, and even our emotions were created to help us to glorify God.

"For we are his workmanship, created in Christ Jesus for good works, which God prepared ahead of time for us to do." Ephesians 2:10

Emotions can tell us what matters to us and remind us to love God more than anything else in the world. Emotions help us to enjoy the wonderful things God has given to us.

We can use our emotions for good when we use them to honor God and love others.

In the beginning, mankind was created with emotions, and they were very good.

Adam and Eve were the first man and woman.

They were filled with joy as they lived in the garden of Eden with God.

They loved Him and delighted in spending time with Him.

But then something went very wrong.

Adam and Eve were tempted by an evil serpent to believe a lie.

The serpent lied and told them God was not giving them enough.

He lied again and told them to eat the fruit God told them not to eat so that they could know everything God knows.

Adam and Eve disobeyed God and ate.

Their disobedience brought the curse of sin to all mankind, and God's relationship with His people was broken.

Because of sin, our emotions got mixed up and confused.

Now, our emotions can lead us to dishonor God and hurt other people.

Because of sin, our emotions can be bad.

Because of sin, our emotions can trick us.

Because of sin, our emotions can make us think only about ourselves.

But wait, there's more!

God has a rescue plan in place to save His people from their sin.

He sent His son, Jesus Christ, to make all things new.

Jesus came to make things right.

Jesus came to restore what was broken.

When Jesus came to the world, He came to save us.

He walked in obedience even when He was tempted.

He did not sin.

He was perfect in every way.

Jesus is the only One who could save us from our sins.

So He went to the cross and took on the punishment we should receive.

He did this so we could have a relationship with God again.

JESUS
LOVES YOU
AND ME

The Gospel of
JOHN

God gives us the Bible to learn more about Him and how we should live.

In the Bible, He teaches us how to use our emotions for good. He gives us the wisdom to understand how we feel and how we can respond in a godly way!

God teaches us to use our emotions to love Him and love one another.

Let's look at the emotions we see in the pages of the Bible...

Joy is permanent happiness that comes from God.

God says in Zephaniah 3:17 that He rejoices over us with gladness! He is so happy to be in a relationship with His children.

He gives His children this joy, too.

When we have a relationship with God, our joy can never be taken away.

Joy makes us smile and laugh, dance and celebrate!

Joy helps us to appreciate God's very good gifts.

Joyous people spread happiness to everyone around them!

"But the righteous are glad; they rejoice before God and celebrate with joy!"

Psalm 68:3

Grief is a deep sadness.

God says in the Bible that He was deeply grieved when He saw so many people disobeying and turning away from Him (Genesis 6:6). It made Him sad because He wanted the best for His people, and they didn't want to listen and obey.

We experience grief, too.

We might feel this when we lose someone or something we love.

We might even experience grief when someone hurts our feelings or when we see others hurting.

When we feel grief or sadness, Jesus says we can come to Him, and He will comfort us.

"Blessed are those who mourn, for they shall be comforted." Matthew 5:4

Jealousy is feeling passionate and protective over something that you think belongs to you.

God displays jealousy in Exodus 34:14 saying, "Because the LORD is jealous for his reputation, you are never to bow down to another god. He is a jealous God."

The people were worshiping other gods and idols. God wanted His people to return to worship Him because He is the One True God. God can be jealous because everything belongs to Him, and He is passionate about protecting it!

Jealousy can show us what we really care about and what we want to protect. But for us, jealousy can also lead us to sin when we think something belongs to us and it doesn't.

We might experience jealousy when our best friend starts to make a new friend.

We might feel jealous when someone has something that we want.

Jealousy can make us selfish and make us do and say things that hurt others.

But in the Bible, we are told not to be jealous or proud and instead to be humble and consider others more important than ourselves (Philippians 2:3).

Anger is feeling upset and displeased by something.

God shows anger in the Old Testament when His people continued to rebel against Him and disobey Him. They were not trusting in God to take care of them. This made God angry because He knew He was the only one who could provide for His people.

We get angry, too.

We might get angry when something bad happens or when someone is unkind to us.

We might get angry when something seems wrong or unfair!

But our anger is often not righteous like God's.

Our anger can cause us to sin against God and others.

The Bible tells us in Ephesians 4:26, "Be angry, but do not sin."

If something makes us angry, we can ask God to help us calm down and trust in Him. He can replace our anger with patience and kindness and help us not to respond sinfully.

Love is an expression of deep care for someone or something.

God shows His love for us in many ways! His greatest display of love for us was sending Jesus to rescue us from our sins so that we could have a relationship with Him forever.

John 3:16 says, "For God loved the world in this way: He gave His one and only Son, so that everyone who believes in Him will not perish but have eternal life."

We experience love, too.

We love our family, and we want to show them how much we care!

We love our friends and our pets.

We can even love books, food, adventures, and holidays!

We love people and things that matter to us.

In the Bible, we are reminded to love each other as God loves us (John 15:12).

God is the perfect example of love, and He helps us to love like Him!

Did you know God knows everything about us?

He knows every little detail because He is our Creator!

He knows everything we feel before we even feel it!

He can understand where our emotions are coming from and why we feel them.

Even if we don't always understand our emotions, we can trust God to help us as we think about our emotions.

Let's look at a few more emotions that we may experience!

Fear is when we don't want something to happen because we think it might harm us or make us uncomfortable.

Fear can make us worry.

Fear can also protect us!

We might feel fear when something looks too dangerous.

We might feel fear when we have to speak in front of our entire class.

We might feel fear when jumping off of a tall diving board.

We might even feel fear when we are about to try something new!

When fear makes us worry, we can pray and ask God to help us trust Him.

He promises to be with us wherever we go and to never leave us.

"God is our refuge and strength, a helper who is always found in times of trouble." Psalm 46:1

Guilt is what we feel when we think we've done something wrong.

You might feel guilty about failing a test and wishing you would have studied more.

You might feel guilty when you do something your parents told you not to do.

You might even feel guilty when a friend is excluded at the playground.

Feeling guilty can actually help us learn from our mistakes.

Guilt can lead us to apologize and ask for forgiveness.

The Bible tells us if we confess our sins, God is faithful to forgive us (1 John 1:9).

If we know we've done something wrong, we do not have to hide it or lie about it.

We can be honest with others and with God, and He promises to forgive us.

Hope is what we feel when we are looking forward to something or wishing something will happen.

We may hope for a new puppy.

We may hope for a snow day!

We may even hope to have a fun and exciting birthday party with all of our friends.

We probably hope for a lot of different things. Some of those things may happen, but some may not.

The Bible tells us about a hope that will never disappoint us, and that is the hope that we find in Jesus! Jesus says if we trust in Him as our Savior, we can be with Him now and forever!

That means we will one day be with Him in heaven, and we will be perfect in every way.

We feel emotions every day.

Some are good, and some are bad.
Some help us, and some hurt us.

We need help to figure out what to do with
our emotions.
Thankfully, God gives us the Bible to teach us
how to live and obey Him in everything we do.

God's Word shapes our hearts and gives
us wisdom.
Everything we feel tells us what is going on
in our hearts.
When we love God more than anything else,
our hearts will show that through our emotions.

When our hearts are changed by God's Word:
Our emotions can help us instead of hurt us.
Our emotions can help us serve and love others.
Our emotions can help us honor and glorify God!

When our hearts are filled with truth from the
Bible, God can use our emotions for good.

God makes a promise to all of His children.

He promises to make them more like Jesus every single day.

He promises to help them fight sin with Spirit and Truth.

He promises to one day change their emotions to be what He wants them to be!

In heaven, our emotions won't confuse us or trick us anymore; they won't lead us to hurt others or sin against God. Isn't that great news!?

Instead, our emotions will help us to enjoy all of God's wonderful gifts and celebrate His creation. Our emotions will help us to love God with all of our hearts and worship Him forever! What an exciting day that will be!